The
HEARTBEAT
of
GOD

Finding the Sacred
in the Middle of Everything
LEADER'S GUIDE

Jenifer Gamber

Walking Together, Finding the Way®
SKYLIGHT PATHS®
PUBLISHING
Nashville, Tennessee

The Heartbeat of God: Finding the Sacred in the Middle of Everything Leader's Guide

ISBN-13: 978-1-59473-308-6 (pbk)
ISBN-13: 978-1-68336-377-4 (hc)

Walking Together, Finding the Way®
Published by SkyLight Paths Publishing
A Division of Longhill Partners, Inc.
AnImprintofTurnerPublishingCompany
4507CharlotteAvenue,Suite100
Nashville,TN37209
Tel:(615)255-2665
www.skylightpaths.com

Contents

Introduction   v

Serving the Poor   1

Healing for All   4

Listening for the Voice of God   6

Creative Survival   8

Opening Doors to Women   10

Seeking Our Roots   12

Peace Work   14

Immigration and Faith   16

Salt of the Earth   18

Heaven on Earth   20

Blessed Are the Change Makers   22

Provoking Love   24

Interrupting Business as Usual   26

Mission Possible   28

Ubuntu   30

God on the Gulf Coast   32

Science and Faith   34

The Ecology of Faith   36

Good Shepherd   38

Who Is Jesus in the World Today?   40

Finding Our Way Home   42

Stardust	45
The Dream of God	47
Called by Name	49
The Web of Life	51
Saints and Superheroes	53
Holy Conversation	55
Practicing Peace	57
Pentecost Continues	59
Living the Questions	61
High Anxiety	63
Pushing the Boundaries	65
Go Forth for God	67
Fossils	69
A Moveable Feast	71
Healing Division	73
Finding God in Dissent	75

Introduction

In this book, Katharine Jefferts Schori addresses issues of justice that are common to all faiths. A dream shared by all faiths is good stewardship of creation, whether it is caring for the earth, fish in the sea, birds of the air, snakes of the ground, and all creeping things or our neighbors. We dream of a world in which people do not hunger, the prisoners are set free, the world is at peace, and the environment is not harmed. The Judeo-Christian tradition describes it this way:

> They shall build houses and inhabit them;
> they shall plant vineyards and eat their fruit.
> They shall not build and another inhabit;
> they shall not plant and another eat.
>
> —Isaiah 65:21–22

The Qur'an exhorts all to follow the way of justice:

> O you who believe! Stand out firmly for justice, as witnesses to Allah, even though it be against yourselves, or your parents, or your kin, be he rich or poor, Allah is a Better Protector to both (than you). So follow not the lusts (of your hearts), lest you may avoid justice, and if you distort your witness or refuse to give it, verily, Allah is Ever Well-Acquainted with what you do.
>
> —Surah 4:35

This leader's guide is intended to help readers reflect on the issues of justice raised by Jefferts Schori. It can be used either with a group through conversation or alone with a journal. While the guide is written from a Christian perspective, people from all faiths will find questions that are appropriate to their concerns. I also encourage you to bring your own experience, sacred texts, and history of your tradition to the conversation. Every religious tradition has a unique perspective. We have much to learn from one another about the human condition and how we might live together in peace and with justice.

Each chapter of the leader's guide is structured in this way:

Scripture References list verses in the Hebrew and Christian Scriptures cited in the chapter in the book. (If there are no scripture references provided, it is because none were specifically addressed in that chapter of the book.) If you are interested in reading and reflecting upon a passage as a group or to understand the greater context of the verse, this will serve as a guide.

Opening and **Closing Prayers** begin and end a study with a ritual that sets aside this time as sacred. These prayers are written by people whose lives reflect a value of justice and take the form of poetry, litanies, and simple prayers.

Discussion Questions can guide a conversation within a group or prompt journaling by an individual. Your reading of the chapter might prompt different avenues for inquiry. Follow your heart and what captures your attention.

Resources is a sampling of just a few books, websites, and videos that relate to the themes in this chapter. However, no list of resources is exhaustive. If you are leading a group you might brainstorm resources to incorporate into your time together. Or you might ask participants to bring in books, videos, and a list of websites they would like to explore. Doing so in an interfaith group will be particularly fruitful.

Jefferts Schori's short, provocative chapters prompt an exploration of a variety of social justice issues. Each of us brings our own perspective and our own contexts to the book. As such, readers will come to different learnings and insights. This book is based on Jefferts Schori's experience. I invite you to share your own experience of addressing hunger, poverty, degradation of the earth, war, homelessness, and other ways in which our world is broken.

Serving the Poor

SCRIPTURE REFERENCES

Genesis 1:31	Isaiah 25:6–7	Matthew 25:34–35
Exodus 22:25–27	Amos 5:24	John 13: 34
Leviticus 19:15	Micah 6:8	Luke 4:17–20
Deuteronomy 15:7	Matthew 4:23	Luke 4:21
Psalm 34:11	Matthew 8:20	Revelation 21:1–3
Isaiah 58:10		

OPENING

Exiting the freeway,
about to enter a business strip,
two lanes, right on red.
No pedestrians allowed.
She is hidden by the car, on my right.
I disturb the accelerator, she darts across.
Frightened, both she and I.
No pedestrians allowed.
I am righteous, defensive, angry.

How can I be?
She's walking home, by foot
from her minimum-wage job
at the Lehigh Valley Mall.
I'm driving home, on wheels,
from a week of vacation
at the Jersey shore.

No pedestrians allowed.

DISCUSSION QUESTIONS

1. Which of the issues mentioned in this chapter—hunger, clean water, homelessness, finance and employment, education, cultural justice, health, environment—are you active in addressing? Which affects you the most?

2. Jefferts Schori talks about boundary crossing. What does boundary crossing mean? Why is it important to justice? Can justice prevail without it? Why or why not?

3. How is access important to justice? What are the limitations of access to addressing these issues?

4. *Write each Scripture cited in the chapter on a separate index card—enough so that each participant has one (duplicates may be necessary). Pass them out randomly.*

    What does the passage you are holding mean to you?

5. *Read Acts 2:43–47 aloud once to the participants.*

    What word or phrase captures your attention?

    Read it aloud a second time.

    What does the word or phrase mean to you?

    Read the passage aloud a third time.

    What is God asking you to do today or this week?

CLOSING

I've received welfare
for the past 30 years.
Middle-class welfare.
Tax relief for my mortgage.

Many others on welfare
don't own a house.
Can't get a job.
Don't have enough food.
Children deprived.

Do I deserve my welfare,
and they not theirs?
They deserve more.

They deserve justice,

and receive only charity.

Opening and Closing by Bill Lewellis, canon theologian, Diocese of Bethlehem

RESOURCES

Just Eating? Practicing Our Faith at the Table (www.practicingourfaith.org), Health Care's Congregational Health Partnerships program, the Northern Illinois Region of Church World Service (CWS), and Presbyterian Church (PCUSA). A six-unit curriculum to explore issues food and faith.

The Meaning of Food (www.pbs.org/opb/meaningoffood), PBS video, 2005. Explores the relationship between food and culture, focusing specifically on the United States.

Millennium Development Goals (www.undp.org/mdg). A global program designed to eliminate extreme poverty by 2015.

Share, Save, Spend (www.sharesavespend.com). A curriculum for adults and children to develop healthy financial habits.

Healing for All

SCRIPTURE REFERENCES

2 Kings 5

Mark 1:40–45

OPENING

You, God, are among us,

The poor, the wealthy and those in between,

In sickness, in health and in homelessness.

Stir in our hearts a passion for justice,

Rouse us to end hunger, poverty and racism.

For you, God, are in the stranger,

You, hungry, poor and homeless once again.

DISCUSSION QUESTIONS

1. Jefferts Schori notes that the literal Greek meaning of the word *compassion* is "gut-wrenched." How might this change your understanding of having compassion for the marginalized?

2. Touch transference is a universal concept in which a person is perceived as being disgusting if they touch a contaminated object or person. Some argue that disgust is an evolutionary response that developed for survival. Does this change your moral judgment of people who have AIDS, or of those who care for them? Why or why not?

3. What diseases or activities do people feel uncomfortable with today? What is the origin of the discomfort? What could be done to get past this fear?

4. Have you, or someone you know, been stigmatized because of your health? How did it make you feel? What did you do in response? Did others support you in addressing the problem? How?

5. Treating people who are ill differently dehumanizes the person who is ill. Might it also dehumanize the person who is acting differently? What does this suggest about wholeness for everyone?

Closing

That our words may be acceptable in your sight,

We entreat you, O Lord.

That victims of crimes may be held in your loving hands,

We entreat you, O Lord.

That prisoners may find their hope in you,

We entreat you, O Lord.

That those on death row may know you and be transformed by your love,

We entreat you, O Lord.

That there may be an end to capital punishment,

We entreat you, O Lord.

That the victims of crime and their families may be healed,

We entreat you, O Lord.

That the guilty may repent of their crimes,

We entreat you, O Lord.

That justice may prevail,

We entreat you, O Lord.

That the families of victims may find in their hearts forgiveness,

We entreat you, O Lord.

That victims, the guilty, and we may be led to compassion and prayer,

We entreat you, O Lord.

Opening and Closing by Joan Findlay Dunham, Society of Companions of the Holy Cross

Resources

AIDS.gov (www.aids.gov). The U.S. government's website that publishes information about AIDS and AIDS public policy.

Five Heroes of AIDS in Africa (www.aidsinafrica.net/5_heroes_hi.php). Streamed online or available for purchase, this documentary by Neil Halloran presents the work of five African activists.

Living with Slim (Sam Kauffman, 2004, 28 min.) samkauffmann.com/films/slim. Interviews of seven African children with HIV/AIDS.

Listening for the Voice of God

SCRIPTURE REFERENCES

1 Samuel 3:1

1 Samuel 3:8–9

Matthew 9:35–38

OPENING

Gracious God, I lift my breath to you that you might hear my cry. A sweet sound, a sound of delight and joy, a sound of the air that passes from heart and lungs through chords to voice, my aching for your presence. Quiet my voice, my heart, and let the air that returns to my body become a rhythm of quiet preparation to hear you.

DISCUSSION QUESTIONS

1. Jefferts Schori recounts a story that appeared in the *Christian Century* about a pastor who built a skate park in the church's backyard. The town prohibited skateboarding in public places and labeled violators juvenile delinquents. Are there people in your community who are diminished by law? Does the church have a role in addressing such laws? What might that role be?

2. What church traditions help you hear God? What traditions might be an obstacle for you? For others? Explain how.

3. Fredrick Buechner says that the place God calls you to is "the place where your deep gladness and the world's deep hunger meet." Where does your deep gladness meet the world's deep hunger? Share a story of when this happened in your life.

4. What does it mean for your community to "give the scriptures and the sacraments and get out of the way?"

5. What truth do you speak with your life? How have others affirmed this for you?

CLOSING

Open my soul, O God, and break through the distractions of my life. Whether your voice comes in rain or wind, in melody of song, in quiet whisper or raging storm, come to me, my God. Give me ears to hear, heart to receive, and hands to respond. Amen.

Opening and Closing by The Very Rev. Anthony R. Pompa, dean and rector,
The Cathedral Church of the Nativity, Bethlehem, Pennsylvania

RESOURCES

Decision Making and Spiritual Discernment: The Sacred Art of Finding Your Way by Nancy L. Bieber (Woodstock, VT: SkyLight Paths, 2010). A companion for staying spiritually grounded and open to divine wisdom as you shape your life. Includes a guide for using the book in groups, with reading assignments, practices, and meditations for each session.

Discerning Your Spiritual Gifts by Lloyd Edward (Cambridge, MA: Cowley Publications, 1988). An expansive presentation of discerning spiritual gifts. Includes exercises for discernment that can be completed in a workshop or group setting.

Sleeping with Bread: Holding What Gives You Life by Dennis Linn, Sheila Fabricant Linn, and Matthew Linn (Mahwah, NJ: Paulist Press, 1995). An accessible introduction to *Examen*—a process of listening to God in everyday life. Suitable for both children and adults.

Creative Survival

SCRIPTURE REFERENCES

Ruth 1:16

Mark 12:41–44

Matthew 1:1–16

OPENING

O God, who wrought creation out of chaos and called it good; embolden us to be present with those who have been taught that their only value is to please and profit others: the poor and elderly shut out of enlivening enterprises; the alien and foreigner accosted by fearful contempt; women and children trafficked for sex. Renew in us all your imaginative hope that, in communion with you and with one another, your creative justice and indiscriminate love may abound in our time. In your most holy name we pray. Amen.

DISCUSSION QUESTIONS

1. Ruth, along with Tamar (who tricks Judah in order to bear a child), Rahab (a prostitute who protected Israelite spies), and Bathsheba, the wife of Uriah (the wife of the soldier King David killed to marry Bathsheba), are included in the genealogy found in the Gospel according to Matthew. Why might these women be included in the genealogy? What does this suggest about the role of women in issues of justice today?

2. How does lack of freedom of the marginalized impact their economic choices? How does this perpetuate inequality? What contributes to this lack of freedom? What evidence do you see of the impact on economic choices? How might your faith community realistically address this problem?

3. How has having access to choices affected your life?

4. How might your understanding of the story of the widow's mite change depending upon whether her giving is the result of generosity or fulfilling the requirement of the temple tax? How might either interpretation matter to your life today?

5. Jefferts Schori says sin is about "removing creative possibility from others, denying them their God-given ability to make choices, to exercise their free will." What are your thoughts about this definition for sin? Would you add to or delete something from the definition? If so, what and why?

6. In what ways do you value people based on what they do? In what ways does society value people in this way? What effects does this have on you and others?

CLOSING

Ever living God, we rejoice in the imaginative actions of Ruth, Naomi, and all whose acts nourished justice and love in their own day, and we thank you for making us in your image, endowing us with creativity, ingenuity, and vision. Open our eyes to the injustices that diminish dignity and steal hope, depriving your children of the freedom to employ creative power. Strengthen our imaginations to sing hope, bring hope, and birth hope for the oppressed in our own day. All this we ask for the sake of the world you are redeeming. Amen.

Opening and Closing by The Rev. E. Claiborne Jones, director and vicar of Emmaus House

RESOURCES

Human Trafficking (www.humantrafficking.org). This web resource for combating human trafficking provides country-specific data and information on public policy to address human trafficking.

Where You Go, I Shall: Gleanings from the Stories of Biblical Widows by Jane J. Parkerton, K. Jeanne Person, and Anne Winchell Silver (Cambridge, MA: Cowley Publications, 2005). First-person accounts of three widows and the issues they face, including financial distress and alienation.

Opening Doors to Women

SCRIPTURE REFERENCES

Psalm 121:1

Isaiah 52:7

Acts 2:1–4

OPENING

O Holy Spirit, the mountains are high, but you are ever close to any who call upon you, give us the strong hearts of your prophets as we follow your lead in our lives of faith and service, in Jesus' name. Amen.

DISCUSSION QUESTIONS

1. Do you remember a time when women were not allowed in church ministry? What were your thoughts and feelings at the time? Do you remember when you first attended a service at which a woman presided? What were your thoughts and feelings at the time? What does this suggest about the contribution of women to ministry?

2. Have you encountered a God-made hill? What were the challenges along the way? What was cause for celebration? From where did your help come?

3. Have you encountered a person-made hill? What were the challenges along the way? What was cause for celebration? From where did your help come?

4. How does oppression "deny the image of God, both in those who are feared and in those who bar the doors"? Share one of your experiences of this.

5. *Read together John 20:19–23.*

   What does this passage mean to you? What might it suggest about closed doors?

CLOSING

O Holy Spirit, you make all things new, give us courage to follow your leading as we open doors unimagined in times gone by. Give us faithful hearts to move mountains and the wisdom of love and humor as companions on the Way, in Jesus' name. Amen.

Opening and Closing by The Rev. Canon Nancy H. Wittig, DMin

RESOURCES

Daughters of the Desert: Stories of Remarkable Women from Christian, Jewish and Muslim Traditions by Claire Rudolf Murphy, Meghan Nuttall Sayres, Mary Cronk Farrell, Sarah Conover, and Betsy Wharton (Woodstock, VT: SkyLight Paths, 2001). A collection of short stories brings to life the women—daring, brave, thoughtful, and wise—who played important and exciting roles in the early days of Judaism, Christianity, and Islam.

Shall We Gather: Anglican Women Together (DVD, 20 min., The Episcopal Church, 2005). This video features interviews of diverse women throughout the world who gathered to learn about and hope for the Beijing Platform for Action.

Women in the Early Church (video, 28 min., Mosaic Television, ELCA, 2004). Tells the story of women in the first three centuries of Christianity. Can be streamed at www2.elca.org/mosaic/ winter04.html.

Women of Color Pray: Voices of Strength, Faith, Healing, Hope and Courage edited and with introductions by Christal M. Jackson (Woodstock, VT: SkyLight Paths, 2003). Prayers by women around the world—from China and Japan, to Syria and Ghana—to African American, Asian American, Native American and Hispanic women in the United States

Women Pray: Voices through the Ages, from Many Faiths, Cultures, and Traditions edited and with introductions by Monica Furlong (Woodstock, VT: SkyLight Paths, 2000). Celebrates the rich variety of ways women around the world have called out to the Divine—with words of joy, praise, gratitude, wonder, petition, longing, and even anger—from the ancient world up to our own day.

Seeking Our Roots

SCRIPTURE REFERENCES

James 2:14–18

OPENING

O God of earth and sky and all who dwell between, who knows when the earth quakes and the sky opens up and when your people are hurting and wandering in search of the Promised Land. Have mercy on those who suffer from nature's fury or the fury of others. Guide us, Lord, and direct our hands and feet to be true servants to all in need.

DISCUSSION QUESTIONS

1. Jefferts Schori says, "brothers and sisters of African heritage in the Episcopal Church continue to lead us toward a world where cries in the wilderness are heard and answered." What does this statement mean to you? How have you listened and answered?

2. Does your community or church support communities in African countries? In light of U.S. history of colonialism, what are the challenges of giving aid? How might those challenges be addressed?

3. In his book *The White Man's Burden* (Oxford: Oxford University Press, 1997), economist William Easterly suggests that foreign aid to African countries is misguided. It creates an incentive to grab more aid instead of focusing on developing healthy internal institutions and markets. And historically, such aid has not been effective. How do you respond?

4. What are the ties that bind the United States to foreign countries? Are some a result of self-interest? Are some due to altruism? Does it make a difference?

CLOSING

We pray to you O Lord, our Father in Heaven,
Who knows the needs of our brothers and sisters throughout the world.

We share the same Father and so truly we are brothers and sisters.
Yet we think and act and believe that some are better than the rest.

Help us to see your all-embracing love for us, your mercy, your kindness.
Open our hearts, Lord, so that we can share your love to all.

Create in us clean hearts O God,
That we may love our neighbors and brothers and sisters as ourselves.

*Opening and Closing by Elizabeth T. Drum, physician team member of
Team Ange, Haiti; Healing the Children, Ethiopia; and Operation
Renewed Hope, Uganda*

RESOURCES

Race: The Power of Illusion (VHS/DVD, 3 parts, 56 min. each, California Newsreel, 2003). Scrutinizes the very idea of race through the distinct lenses of science, history, and our social institutions. Leader guide at www.pbs.org/race.

Peace Work

SCRIPTURE REFERENCES

Luke 19:40

John 14:27

OPENING

Almighty God, you alone know the peace that is possible in this, your Creation. Give us strength and courage to love and serve you, and help us to strive for justice, in order that your glory may be evident to all. Amen.

DISCUSSION QUESTIONS

1. What fears keep you from the blessed road of "joy and peace and abundant life"? What might help you set aside those fears?

2. Who in your community is the gentle, strong, and courageous presence that eases the fear of meeting Jesus among the cries of injustice? How might his or her gift be lifted in your community?

3. What kind of muscles do you need to exercise to join Jesus on the trail?

CLOSING

Grant, O God, that your spirit may be present in each of us, and may embolden our hearts and empower our minds so that, in the pursuit of peace, we might even walk into the jaws of death for the sake of abundant life. Amen.

Opening and Closing by The Rev. Mariclair Partee, cannon for the Ministry of the Baptized, The Cathedral Church of the Nativity, Bethlehem, Pennsylvania

RESOURCES

Fritz Eichenberg: Works of Mercy edited by Robert Ellsberg (Maryknoll, NY: Orbis Books, 1993). Reprints the compelling woodcuts of Fritz Eichenberg, many which are meditations of "Inasmuch as you did these things to the least of my brothers and sisters, you did them to me." Wonderful opportunity to reflect God's call for justice through art.

Immigration and Faith

SCRIPTURE REFERENCES

Leviticus 19:18

Leviticus 19:34

Deuteronomy 10:19

OPENING

I know you, my sisters and brothers. Your parents, like Mary and Joseph, left their homeland and crossed a border to keep you safe. Shalom, my sister, my brother, my neighbor, made in the image of God. May this country, the only homeland you have ever known, the place where you have worked, married, and raised your own family, be a sanctuary, embracing you with love and honoring you as a child of God. In Jesus' name, we pray. Amen.

DISCUSSION QUESTIONS

1. How does Jefferts Schori's "long view" of migration challenge or affirm your position about immigration into the United States?

2. Share your spiritual migration through an event—either recent or a long time ago. What borders did you cross? How has it shaped you today?

3. Welcoming the alien traveler was a matter of life and death in ancient Israel. The story of the Oaks of Mamre (Genesis 18:1–15) tells of Abram's radical hospitality. What blessing did Sarah and Abram receive from their hospitality? What do we share with that story today?

4. Who are the foreigners in your community? How are they welcomed?

5. The Episcopal House of Bishops met in Phoenix in September 2010 in solidarity with immigrants there. How might you express solidarity with immigrants?

CLOSING

Father, your love knows no borders, no boundaries. Break down the fences of fear, the walls of ignorance, and the towers of hatred that blind us. Dazzle us with the light of your mercy so that our hearts and minds become shining sanctuaries of welcome for all your children. In Jesus' name, we pray.

Opening and Closing by Jan H. Logan, Society of the Companions of the Holy Cross

RESOURCES

Christians for Comprehensive Immigration Reform (www.faithandimmigration.org). This web resource, created by a coalition of Christian organizations, churches, and leaders from across the theological and political spectrum, provides updates about immigration reform and resources for discussing immigration in faith communities. This site also provides leader's guides for the four films listed below.

Dying to Live: A Migrant's Journey (DVD, 33 min., The Center for Latino Spirituality and Culture, University of Notre Dame). This documentary looks at immigration across the U.S-Mexico border through personal stories and reflections by photographers, theologians, congressional leaders, activists, musicians, and immigrants. A discussion guide is available at dyingtolive.nd.edu.

Made in L.A. (DVD, 70 min.). This documentary follows the stories of three undocumented workers who join a grassroots organization and fight for and win basic labor protection. A "Delve Deeper" guide is available at www.madeinla.com.

Strangers No Longer (DVD, 16 or 22 min., Justice for Immigrants Campaign). This documentary connects immigration today with immigration throughout U.S. history and examines potential solutions to current problems. A discussion guide is available at www.dyingtolive.nd.edu/other.html.

The Visitor (DVD, 104 min., www.thevisitorfilm.com). This drama shares one man's transformation housing immigrants and negotiating the immigration deportation system.

Salt of the Earth

SCRIPTURE REFERENCES

Genesis 19:20–26   Matthew 23:33

Amos 3:12, 4:1   John 15:15

Matthew 5:13–14

OPENING

God, I crave the taste of salt, just enough to help my meal taste good. But I hear that you wish for me to be the salt of the earth. What gifts or character do I have to help me help others or to be seen as salt of the earth? What possible salt do I bring to enliven the spirits of fellow sojourners or to preserve what needs to be preserved or to spice up a meal of conversation? Help me to mine the salt that is within me and around me so that I might see clearly or see at all that which needs to be treasured and given new life.

DISCUSSION QUESTIONS

1. What role does the metaphor of salt play in your life? Do you need more or less? Or is the amount just right? Why?

2. Jefferts Schori reminds us that salt is part of who we are as human beings and that in the ancient Middle East it was considered as valuable as gold. How might these two facts change your view of costly living?

3. *Read together Mark 9:45–50.* What might salt mean in this passage? What does it suggest about your life?

4. What are the attributes of salt? What does each attribute suggest about what is required to do justice?

5. Where do you need a pinch of salt to bring out the seasonings of your life?

CLOSING

How will I know the amount of salt that is needed or that which is too much or harmful? Help me to trust that you know the answers to these questions and know other questions that I should be asking. I sense that I am not being called to be a lump of salt or to be too intrusive, as salt, in the lives of others. But I believe that I am called to engage the real stuff of living. Help me, O God, in my believing and in my disbelieving, in my saltiness and in my blandness, in my being and in my doing, so that I might be open to being engaged in the life you have prepared for me and others at the beginning of creation and in its ongoing unfolding. Amen.

Bud Holland, priest, Diocese of Pennsylvania

Heaven on Earth

SCRIPTURE REFERENCES

Deuteronomy 6:5

Matthew 5:1–12

OPENING

Help us.

Help us not to fear.

Help us to know our inter-relatedness

with one another and all being and all life.

Help us not to separate, destroy, corrupt,

divide, or shun Your creation.

Awaken us!

Help us to know our need of You.

Your kingdom come

Your will be done

On earth as in heaven.

DISCUSSION QUESTIONS

1. Jefferts Schori tells us that to be poor in spirit means "not lording it over somebody else … not playing games of in and out, acceptable and despicable." Jesus tells us that "theirs is the kingdom of God." Why might this phrase begin the beatitudes?

2. What does the dream of God look like to you? What are the signs of the birth of that kingdom in the world today?

3. The origin of the word *passion* means "to suffer." It was not until the sixteenth century that it was used in reference to sexual love. What does seeing your passions as gifts by God suggest about what you follow?

4. What might you have to give up to fulfill God's dream of the kingdom of heaven on earth?

5. In her book, *The Dream of God,* Verna Dozier says that we are not called to worship Jesus, but rather to follow Jesus. How does this challenge your sense of being Christian? What is the meaning of worship in this context?

CLOSING

Help us.

Help us to dream your dream.

Draw us fully into the passion of your heart

For it is your good pleasure to give us the kingdom!

Your kingdom come

Your will be done

On earth as in heaven.

Opening and Closing by Suzanne Guthrie, www.edgeofenclosure.org

RESOURCES

God's Dream by Archbishop Desmond Tutu and Douglas Carlton Abrams (Somerville, MA: Candlewick, 2008). Shares the joy of reconciliation through the story of two children who get in a fight. For ages 4–8.

Living into Hope: A Call to Spiritual Action for Such a Time as This by Rev. Dr. Joan Brown Campbell; foreword by Karen Armstrong (Woodstock, VT: SkyLight Paths, 2010). Speaks out on the pressing issues that face us today: love, justice, reconciliation, forgiveness and community. Includes extensive discussion guide by Jenifer Gamber and The Rev. Mariclair Partee.

Pyramid Professional Resources (www.pprlex.org). Provides "encouragement, mentoring, and support" to the homeless in Lexington, Kentucky, so that they might break the boundaries that limit their lives.

Blessed Are the Change Makers

Scripture References

Hebrews 10:24

Opening

Loving God, many things make me afraid. Change is one of them. Yet I hear your voice and feel your hand leading me from fear to life. Your voice calls me to repentance. Your love calls me to change. Your life calls me to abundant life.

And so I praise your holy name.

Give me the daily grace I need to turn and change my ways. Give me the daily love I need to live in compassionate ways. Help me speak truth to power. Help me be your love today. Help me to do the things I can and to be your light each day. Give me courage to face each day knowing your call to eternal life. You are my hope, you are my love and the change I need is in your hands.

And so I put all my desires and my desire for change into your loving care.

Discussion Questions

1. What provokes you to proclaim the good news?

2. *Read together Matthew 5:3–10.* In which of these beatitudes do you most live out your ministry? Can you identify others who live them out differently than you?

3. What transitions have you experienced, or would you anticipate, as God's kingdom breaks into the world? What have been, or will be, the costs of these transitions?

4. What challenges do you face living God's rules when the rules of others are inconsistent with God's rules? Which are most important? Which might you address another day?

5. Jefferts Schori mentions health care and climate change as issues the world most needs to address now. What issues do you believe need to be addressed and require the most change?

CLOSING

Dear Lord, hold my life and hold my heart. Hold my mind and hold my soul. Hold my nights and hold my days. Hold the changing of my ways.

Grant me grace when things change and I have no control over them. Grant me strength and faith.

When I need to change, when I need to embrace a new path, when I need to speak a new word or do a new act, grant me your love to know that you stand with me through all the changes of this life.

Change me. Change my heart, my mind and soul. Change me only if it brings your glory. Change me only if it fulfills your will. Change me if I become the child and love you want me to be.

Opening and Closing by The Rev. Mark Bozzuti-Jones, priest for pastoral care, Trinity, Wall Street, New York

RESOURCES

Contemplating God Changing the World by Mario I. Aguilar (New York: Seabury Books, 2008). Tells the story of contemporary people of faith whose prayer lives prompted and supported their acts of justice. Included are Thomas Merton, Ernesto Cardenal, Daniel Berrigan, Sheila Cassidy, Desmond Tutu, and Mother Teresa.

Living the Lord's Prayer by Archbishop Rowan Williams and Sister Wendy Beckett (Oxford, UK: Lion, 2007). Looks at the meaning behind the words in the Lord's Prayer along with examples of how it has impacted lives.

Ten Amazing People: And How They Changed the World by Maura D. Shaw; full-color illus. by Stephen Marchesi; foreword by Dr. Robert Coles (Woodstock, VT: SkyLight Paths, 2002). Shows kids that spiritual people can have an exciting impact on the world around them. Includes activities.

Provoking Love

Scripture References

Matthew 3:17

John 3:5

John 3:16

John 4:11–13

Romans 8:16

Opening

Holy Creator of the universe and all its wondrous mysteries, we thank you for your boundless love as experienced in the works of creation. Grant us the endurance to walk along side you in the way of love. When we stumble and fail to love without obligation, help us to stand and regain our footing once again. As wind ignites a slow-burning fire, breathe your spirit across our hearts and ignite the passion for love and justice that resides within our bodies so that we may continue your work on this earth. Through Jesus Christ our Lord, Amen.

Discussion Questions

1. What is the difference between telling the good news and being the good news? What is the good news? Is it the same for all people or is it different depending on a person's life experience and status in life?

2. What sacramental sign outside the church have you seen recently that says someone loves you? How did it make you feel? Did it prompt a response?

3. What does your baptism mean to you? Does it change who you are? If so, in what way?

4. *The Message* version of John 3:16 asks whether God sent his son merely "to point an accusing finger, telling the world how bad it is." What is the temptation to point an accusing finger? How is pointing an accusing finger harmful? Is it ever helpful?

CLOSING

Gracious God, who makes all things *real*, we praise you for another day among your creation. In moments that are both mundane and sublime, help us to recognize your face in ourselves, in those that we know best, and in the stranger among us. Continue to open our eyes to your infinite love as revealed in our own ability to love endlessly. Free us from the prison of fear and ignorance so that we may contribute wholly as members of earth's community. Through Jesus our Lord, Amen.

Opening and Closing by Melissa A. Robinson

RESOURCES

Poarch Band of Creek Indians (www.poarchcreekindians-nsn.gov). A website about the Creek Indians.

"We Shall Be Free" from *The Chase* by Garth Brooks (Pearl Records, 2007). A song about how freedom is when the hungry are fed, the oceans are clean, and the homeless have shelter. Reflecting on lyrics is a source of insights into culture and beliefs.

Interrupting Business as Usual

SCRIPTURE REFERENCES

Luke 4:18–21

Luke 9:1–6

Luke 23:43

OPENING

O God of abundance, you feed us every day; rise in us now and make us into your bread that we may share your gifts with a hungry world and join in love with all people through Jesus Christ our Lord. Amen.

DISCUSSION QUESTIONS

1. Jesus tells his disciples to take nothing for the journey to preach the kingdom of God. What baggage is weighing you down? How might you let it go?

2. When have you had to "shake the dust off your feet" because the people did not welcome you? How did it feel to be unwelcomed? How did it feel to shake the dust off your feet or have you yet to do so?

3. What interruptions in your day, week, or year have revealed God's grace?

4. Jefferts Schori uses the words "co-creating with God." What does co-creating with God mean? Does it challenge or affirm your understanding of a relationship with God? Explain.

5. How can you interrupt the days of others to "remind everyone of the abundance around us"?

CLOSING

I wasn't expecting you to be here, not in this everyday place. You were supposed to be safely away—in light inaccessible and hid from me. But then you came into view in the most unexpected and ordinary way I could imagine. You touched my life and healed my vision so that all I could see was filled with your presence: you in the child and the criminal; you in the lover and the stranger; you in the healer and in the hurt. In all of these faces and a thousand others you came to me and made me new. And so I give you unceasing praise, God my creator. Amen.

Opening from the Food Pantry at St. Gregory of Nyssa, by Sara Miles

Closing by The Rev. Paul D. Fromberg, rector, St. Gregory of Nyssa, San Francisco, California, 2010

RESOURCES

Free Hugs Campaign (www.freehugscampaign.org). Learn about how the movement was started and how to join. Includes a video showing the reactions of people on the street to someone giving out free hugs.

Giving—The Sacred Art: Creating a Lifestyle of Generosity by Lauren Tyler Wright (Woodstock, VT: SkyLight Paths, 2008). Explores the practices of generosity that spiritually renew and transform our lives.

How Much Is Enough? by Arthur Simon (Grand Rapids, MI: Baker Books, 2003). Takes a critical look at not just the hollowness but the harm of a life of continual acquisition.

Mission Possible

Scripture References

Matthew 10:5–13

Luke 10:4

Ephesians 2:19

Opening

Holy Lord, as we acknowledge your presence among us, so interrupt our thoughts, our habits, and our personal desires, that in our discussion and sharing our hearts may be flooded with the urgency to go and be your missionaries wherever you send us. This we ask in the name of Jesus, your missionary to us. Amen.

Discussion Questions

1. When have you last seen the image of God in a person you have met? What did you see?

2. Are you ready to be sent by Jesus? What would (or does) keep you from going?

3. Does your church bring the scripture and the sacraments and then get out of the way? If so, how? If not, what might the church look like if it did?

4. What institutional structures do you rely on? (Some examples are the legal code in a country, the hierarchy in a corporation, and the rules and worship practices of a church, synagogue, or temple.) What would it mean to rely less on those structures?

5. How might you announce peace at your place of work? Or to the communities that you serve?

Closing

Lord God, Creator and Great Provider, make us sacraments of your love and mercy. Help us to let go of the hindrances that serve as closed shutters to your grace, that we might open ourselves to give and to receive the unexpected surprises that bring healing and peace, light and life, and the fulfillment of your kingdom on earth. We pray in the name of Him who gives us life, even Jesus Christ, our Lord and only Savior. Amen.

Opening and Closing by Laura Drum, Society of the Companions of the Holy Cross

RESOURCES

Lifting Women's Voices: Prayers to Change the World edited by Margaret Rose, Jeanne Person, Abagail Nelson, and Jenny Te Paa (New York: Morehouse, 2009). Prayers by women around the world to address the Millennium Development Goals.

Simple Ways: Toward the Sacred by Gunilla Norris (Mamaronek, NY: Bluebridge, 2008). Offers reflections toward noticing the sacred in everyday places and practices.

What Can One Person Do? Faith to Heal a Broken World by Sabina Alkire and Edmund Newell (New York: Church Publishing, 2005). Asks how a person might address the Millennium Development Goals.

Ubuntu

SCRIPTURE REFERENCES

Ezekiel 36:24–35

Ezekiel 37:5

OPENING

Stop

Stop and listen

To the beating

Signaling God's life

All around

His presence we hold dear

Connecting us

All around

Through our own beating heart

To all beating hearts

Please stop

Listen

DISCUSSION QUESTIONS

1. Where has your heart hardened?

2. Have you experienced "new life that comes from living in a new way"? If so, what has it been like? If not, what new way might you take on?

3. Have you ever thought of Jesus as an organ donor? How does this change your view or beliefs?

4. What is your understanding of *ubuntu*? Are there other understandings of personhood? What are they and how do they differ with *ubuntu*? Do the differences matter?

5. Is your faith community in need of a heart transplant? What are signs of generosity? What are signs of withholding?

CLOSING

For some questions
There are no easy answers
No true metaphor to learn
There exist no elements
That exclude all others
In accuracy and precision
Instead you must fight inside
To live with those questions
To learn, to listen, to love fully
Those questions that teach
And in so, find the true admission
Of heart and body and soul

Opening and Closing by Elizabeth Yale, student at Allegheny College

RESOURCES

Ubuntu: I in You and You in Me by Michael Battle (New York: Seabury Books, 2009). Explores what it means that "I am because we are" and how that understanding compels us to love our neighbors.

God on the Gulf Coast

OPENING

Mother of Sea: crashing waves and perilous whirlpools, waterspouts and dark depths, whales and fishes, coral and abalone, kelp and krill, we delight in your love, forgive us and heal us.

DISCUSSION QUESTIONS

1. The tragedy of the commons is that individuals acting out of self-interest will deplete shared resources even though the outcome is deleterious to all. What resources in your community are at risk of this tragedy?

2. What responsibility does BP have in the Gulf oil problem? What responsibility do consumers of oil have?

3. What responsibility does the church have to respond to the Gulf oil problem? What might that response look like?

4. The sin by one has rippling effects throughout the community. Why is this so? What role might the community play in addressing that sin?

5. Consider a day in your life. Name a few actions and how they impacted those around you and perhaps even those afar. Is this impact positive or negative?

CLOSING

Mother of Water: swollen river and raging flood, swampy wetlands, fountains of crystal waters, lakes and ponds and aquifers, we delight in your love, forgive us and heal us.

Prayers from Litany of the Earth *by Sister Catherine Grace, Community of the Holy Spirit in Brewster, New York*

RESOURCES

Genesis Farm (www.genesisfarm.org). Offers workshops in re-imagining ourselves as part of the cosmos and creation.

The Universe Story: From the Primordial Flaring Forth to the Ecozoic Era—A Celebration of the Unfolding of the Cosmos by Brian Swimme (New York: HarperOne, 1994). Explores the evolution of life on earth and the interconnectedness of all creation.

Science and Faith

OPENING

Holy One, your triune life points your creatures toward our need to be united one to another in love, care and concern for each other. Give us hearts to see the deep connections present in the webs of life and the ways actions can have effects we cannot foresee. Grant us the grace of humility as we live into the mystery of a common life whose boundaries we barely discern. Amen.

DISCUSSION QUESTIONS

1. How does what you choose affect the web of life?

2. An ocean is a collection of millions of drops of water. Explore this image and what it contributes to the message in this chapter.

3. How does your community value and encourage truth telling?

4. How might you apply what you have learned in your work life—either paid or unpaid—to understanding the One who has blessed us with memory, reason, and skill?

5. If society values actions that minimize harm, why do we disagree about policy? What does this suggest about the role of faith communities to developing public policy?

CLOSING

Almighty God, you blessed us with memory, reason, and skill. We use these gifts to behold the bounds of the heavens, the beginnings of time, the dances of particles, and the swells of the quantum foam. We have used them to unleash shattering explosions, ignite the air, scour the coasts, and befoul your creation. Let your Holy Wisdom guide us in our use of the gifts you have given us that we might ever explore and never again destroy. Amen.

Opening and Closing by The Very Rev. Nicholas Knisely, dean, Trinity Cathedral, Phoenix, Arizona

RESOURCES

Claiming Earth as Common Ground: The Ecological Crisis through the Lens of Faith by Andrea Cohen-Kiener; foreword by Rev. Sally Bingham (Woodstock, VT: SkyLight Paths, 2009). Gathers insights from ecology coalitions, emerging theologies, and spiritual and environmental activists to rally and inspire us to work across denominational lines in order to fulfill our sacred imperative to care for God's creation.

To Serve and Guard the Earth: God's Creation Story and Our Environmental Concern by Beth Bojarski (New York: Church Publishing, 2010). Through six sessions, participants learn about the theology of creation, understanding about the environment and the opportunity to change actions to address today's environmental concerns.

The Ecology of Faith

SCRIPTURE REFERENCES

Jeremiah 17:7–8

Mark 10:34–45

Luke 3:21–22

John 4:6–15

OPENING

Good Shepherd, who knows each creature as your beloved, we thank you for cupping creation in the palm of your hand. Relax our hands so that we may let go of our need to control this world that we are forever and continuously born into. Lighten our feet so that we may walk in concert with you and the home that you have provided. Unplug our ears and help us to hear your voice in every rock, river, and creature that we fail to see. Open our mouths and give us the breath to sing in harmony with the diversity of your creation. Through your son, Jesus. Amen.

DISCUSSION QUESTIONS

1. How are you connected to the water of life? What are the ways in which you drink from this water?

2. Can you remember a time when you took a "deep breath of life"? Share the experience.

3. Consider times when you felt beloved and when you did not receive love. How did each change your view of the world and your place in it?

4. What do you do to deepen your roots into the source of life?

5. From what waters do you drink? What characterizes that water?

6. What are the challenges to moving from a model of competition and scarcity to one of sacrifice and abundance?

CLOSING

Great Creator, in you we forever find the source of true life. As we squint our eyes searching the heavens or dirty our palms discovering what lies beneath, remind us of the baptismal hope that in your works we are infused with wonder and awe. Let us not forget that it is in our mud-caked knuckles, grass-stained knees, and water-logged skin that we are born again into a life with you and your creation. Through Jesus Christ our Lord. Amen.

Opening and Closing Prayers by Melissa A. Robinson

RESOURCES

The Center for Compassion and Altruism Research (www.ccare.stanford.edu). A community of neuroscientists, psychologists, economists, and contemplative scholars to seek to understand compassion and its roots.

Loosening the Roots of Compassion: Meditations for Holy Week and Eastertide by Ellen Bradshaw Aitken (Cambridge, MA: Cowley Publications, 2006). Takes you on the journey through Holy Week and Eastertide, loosening compassion in your life.

The Sacred Art of Lovingkindness: Preparing to Practice by Rami Shapiro; foreword by Marcia Ford (Woodstock, VT: SkyLight Paths, 2006). Tells us about the practice of compassion and invites us to cultivate lovingkindness in every aspect of our lives—toward ourselves, others, nature, and animals. Includes practical exercises.

Good Shepherd

SCRIPTURE REFERENCES

John 10:14–15

OPENING

God of all, you sent your son to be our shepherd, to care for us together and individually. Help us to recognize his call, to respond in faith and to understand that he loved us enough to give his life for us; through Jesus the true shepherd. Amen.

DISCUSSION QUESTIONS

1. Jefferts Schori talks about different types of leaders. What kind of leader do you need today? Has this kind of leader always served you well? Why or why not?

2. What is the distinctive call of your shepherd?

3. What is the distinctive voice by which your shepherd knows you?

4. Imagine a Hells Angel Jesus or a gang leader Jesus. What would each look like—both physically and in their behavior? How does this image challenge how you see Jesus?

CLOSING

Jesus my shepherd,
If I turn away,
    call me.
So that I feel your closeness,
    name me.
If I cry in my uncertainty,
    hear me.
When I fail to recognize the path,
    guide me.

When I lack protection,
>surround me.
Because I need love,
>enfold me.
Amen.

*Opening and Closing by Deacon Lynn V. Rutledge, Christ Episcopal Church,
Eastport, Maine*

RESOURCES

God the What? *What Our Metaphors for God Reveal about Our Beliefs in God* by Carolyn Jane Bohler (Woodstock, VT: SkyLight Paths, 2009). Challenges our common images of God by blowing the lid off conventional God-descriptors. Inspires you to consider a wide range of images of God in order to refine how you imagine God to have and use power, and how God wills and makes divine will happen—or not.

The Long Loneliness by Dorothy Day (New York: HarperOne, 1996). Day's autobiography, a life dedicated to working for and among the poor, the oppressed and the voiceless.

Who Is Jesus in the World Today?

SCRIPTURE REFERENCES

Mark 2:1–12   Luke 4:21

Mark 5:3   John 14:6

Mark 5:25–29   Romans 8:31–39

Mark 10:38

OPENING

Now there was leaning on Jesus' bosom one of his disciples, whom Jesus loved. Simon Peter therefore beckoned to him, that he should ask who it should be of whom he spake. He then lying on Jesus' breast saith unto him, Lord, who is it?

–John 13:23–25 (KJV)

Tiny star
of morning.
Born in the
smallest of stables
spreading from manger
to shepherd
to magi
to beloved
to teacher.
Expanding out
into the universe.
Calling everyone and everything
home to the heart of Love.
Transfiguration reveals
what was always there:
A supernova exploding

into our hearts and minds.

Now we feel the black hole

DISCUSSION QUESTIONS

1. Do you agree that the ministry of presence also means absence? How might that be true? How might it present a challenge?

2. What drumming song of compassion do you hear?

3. What have you encountered while on retreat?

4. Jefferts Schori talks about her awe of creation such as squid that never see the light of day and still "put out their own flashes of light." Have you put out flashes of light? Have you received them from others? What have these flashes been like?

5. How have you received the "babe born not to Caesar, in political military might, but to a poor and homeless couple on the run"?

CLOSING

Resting in Christ,

close enough to

hear the heartbeat of God,

drumming a song of compassion

for the creation and all its creatures.

Help me to see with your eyes of love

as I go out into your world each day.

Opening and Closing by The Rev. Ann Fontaine, author of Streams of
Mercy: A Meditative Commentary on the Bible
(www.authorhouse.com)

RESOURCES

Being Home: Discovering the Spiritual in the Everyday by Gunilla Norris and Greta Sibley (Mahwah, NJ: HiddenSpring, 2001). This brief book of reflections invites you to a practice of mindfulness during every hour of what appear to be ordinary days.

Divine Proportion: Phi in Art, Nature and Science by Priya Hemenway (New York: Sterling Publishing, 2005). Invites you to see the beauty of the divine mysteries of creation.

Finding Our Way Home

SCRIPTURE REFERENCES

John 10:1–2

John 10:14–18

OPENING

Almighty God, who through your Son Jesus, the Good Shepherd, calls us each by name: Open our hearts to your boundless love that we, knowing we are all both sheep and shepherds, may come to hear the cries of those in fear or pain and gently tend them with your gifts of justice and mercy; through Jesus our Lord, who lives and reigns with you and the Holy Spirit, one God, now and forever. Amen.

DISCUSSION QUESTIONS

1. What does the metaphor of the herd that needs to keep moving to remain healthy mean to you? What does it suggest about your ministry?

2. What does it mean to be "known by name"? What difference does it make to how a person sees his or her place in the world?

3. Through what prisms have you known the Lord? What insights have you gained from the many ways to see God?

4. In what distance meadows have you grazed? How has that impacted your life and ministry?

5. Explore the metaphor of the sheep and its shepherd. What does it say to you? While a common activity in Jesus' time, not many in the United States today tend sheep. What contemporary metaphor might capture the same message?

CLOSING

Leader: Let us pray to you, O God, for faith and for courage, that, with your grace, we may find our way home, saying, "Hear our prayer."

Leader: For all who seek you, that we may answer your call, throughout the ages, for justice and for mercy; Lord in your mercy,
People: Hear our prayer.

Leader: For acceptance and respect among people of all faiths, that we shall live together in dignity and peace; Lord in your mercy,
People: Hear our prayer.

Leader: For dialogue and understanding within your Church, that we will work together to love and serve you; Lord in your mercy,
People: Hear our prayer.

Leader: For coming to know you anew through different prisms and diverse lenses, that we may reject petty differences and embrace your fullness; Lord in your mercy,
People: Hear our prayer.

Leader: For a spirit of wisdom to heed the two great commands, that where there is prejudice and oppression, we will be present, remain watchful, and tell the hard truth; Lord in your mercy,
People: Hear our prayer.

Leader: For pastoral ministries that take us from our comfort and into the world, that we may choose the path that leads to broader meadows and home to you; Lord in your mercy,
People: Hear our prayer.

Leader: O God, our Redeemer and Protector, listen to the prayers of your people, that we may truly receive your Word and become one with Jesus our Lord, in this world and in the world to come. We ask all this through your blessed Son, Lamb of God and Shepherd of your flock.

Opening and Closing by Elizabeth H. House, executive director of Grace Montessori School, Grace Episcopal Church, Allentown, Pennsylvania

RESOURCES

The Irresistible Revolution: Living as an Ordinary Radical by Shane Claiborne; foreword by Jim Wallis (Grand Rapids, MI: Zondervan, 2006). Shares the commitment of Shane Claiborne to live as Jesus did, among and serving the poor and homeless.

The Shepherd and the 100 Sheep by Michal Hudak (Collegeville, MN: The Liturgical Press, 1998). This whimsical book tells the story of the Good Shepherd who leaves the flock to search for little Wooly who had woken up on the wrong side of the bed and wandered away from the fold. Although written for elementary age children, the book is insightful even for adults.

Stardust

OPENING

A cross of oil marks us as Christ's own forever.

And still we forget.

A cross of ashes reminds us who we are, and whose we are:

Almighty God, you have created us out of the dust of the earth and the stars to be your people. Help us to remember that we belong to you, and in your great love for us, you have made us forever yours, on earth and in heaven, through Jesus our Lord and Savior. Amen.

DISCUSSION QUESTIONS

1. How does remembering "to dust you shall return" influence your life?

2. Do you hear the words "From dust you came, and to dust you shall return" differently when you replace the word "dust" to "stardust?" How? What is lost in the meaning of the phrase when you do so? What is gained?

3. Have you ever considered that your heart has an ear? What does it mean for your heart to have an ear?

4. How do you define prayer?

5. What prayer practices help you to hear with your heart? What do you hear?

CLOSING

The heavens declare the glory of God; and the firmament shows God's handiwork.

Everything above me and below me, everything around me
sings of your glory, your truth, your righteousness.

Burn away my secret faults. Leave only what is pure.

Make me wholly yours.

Let me hear and share the message of the stars.

I too will shine as a reflection of your love.

May I listen as you speak, O Lord, and when I speak,

Let the words of my mouth and the meditation of my heart be always acceptable to you, O Lord, my rock and my redeemer.

Opening and Closing by Wendy Claire Barrie, Christian educator

RESOURCES

Celebration of Discipline: The Path to Spiritual Growth by Richard J. Foster (London: Hodder & Stoughton, 1998). Outlines the classic spiritual disciplines.

Seeking God: The Way of St. Benedict by Esther de Waal; foreword by Kathleen Norris (Collegeville, MN: The Liturgical Press). Interprets the rule for people's lives today.

The Dream of God

SCRIPTURE REFERENCES

Matthew 25:40

OPENING

What is this that both nags and stirs, that bolsters and builds in my soul? What is this portrait painted in the dreams of my sleep that moves me to laughter and joy, to tears and heartbreak? What is this melody of life that plays in the core of my being and calls me out to bind to another's heart broken or whole?

DISCUSSION QUESTIONS

1. How do you define *family*?

2. Each of us shares more DNA with people in other ethnic groups than with people in our own ethnic group. What does this suggest about your family?

3. Revisit the Exodus story of the Hebrews from bondage into the land of milk and honey. What images come to mind? How might these images inform our response to what binds others from God's fullness in our time?

4. Eighty percent of Haitians live below the poverty line and 50 percent live in abject poverty. What challenges do Haitians face in developing an economy that would provide sufficiently for all its citizens? What might privileged countries do to help?

CLOSING

What is this courage that rises up within, forcing me to shout to the world when injustice abounds? What is this abiding peace poured deep into the foundation of my life that inexplicably stands firm when the storm seas of life blow hard against it? What is this fiercely beautiful tapestry of grace, hope, and love so wonderfully woven to perfectly fit what our lives and the world can be? Could it be your dream O God? Bless us O God with your dream!

Opening and Closing by The Rev. Anthony R. Pompa, dean and rector, The Cathedral Church of the Nativity, Bethlehem, Pennsylvania

RESOURCES

God Has a Dream: A Vision of Hope for Our Time by Archbishop Desmond Tutu and Douglas Carlton Abrams (New York: Image, 2005). Through stories from his life, Tutu invites readers to see God's love transforming suffering into joy.

Mountains beyond Mountains: The Quest of Dr. Paul Farmer, a Man Who Would Cure the World by Tracy Kidder (New York: Random House, 2009). The story of Paul Farmer's transformative medical work in Haiti.

Called by Name

SCRIPTURE REFERENCES

Job 42:14

Mark 10:46–52

Mark 1:11

OPENING

Good morning, God.

Good morning, my friend.

Who? ME??

Yes, you! Rise and shine! Together we've got places to go, things to do, and good news to share.

DISCUSSION QUESTIONS

1. What is the history of your first name? Your last name? How has this history shaped you?

2. Has being welcomed or called by name ever surprised you? How did it make you feel?

3. What does your community do to encourage members to call one another by name? Are all included in this plan? How has it impacted your community? Newcomers?

4. How would approaching your task hearing the words, "with you I am well pleased" differ from beginning the task with, "I will be pleased with you when your work is done"? How might your work look different in each?

CLOSING

God of grace and goodness, you call me by name to wholeness and health. I call on you as my friend. Lead me on the way.

Opening and Closing by Kay Flores, The Church

RESOURCES

To Bless the Space Between Us: A Book of Blessings by John O'Donohue (New York: Doubleday, 2008). Offers blessings for events in our days and of our lives. Blessing our days and one another creates spaces of belonging and mutuality.

Compassion as a Subversive Activity: Illness, Community, and the Gospel of Mark by David K. Urion (Cambridge, MA: Cowley Publications, 2006). Brings together the experience of a pediatric neurologist and theology to drive the Christian imperative to heal and to welcome the healed.

The Web of Life

Scripture References

Deuteronomy 23:1
Isaiah 53:7–8
Isaiah 56:5
Acts 8:36–40

Opening

Let them see me, my God, today, as more than a silver polisher, nose wiper, linen ironer, muffin maker, bulletin stuffer. Then unlock my fears and push me through the door.

I will serve you, O Lord. Amen

Discussion Questions

1. How does baptism connect a person to the stream of life and the generations?

2. What events in your life have shaped your identity today?

3. How is your life today linked to the lives of your grandparents, great-grandparents or other ancestors?

4. Who is cut off in our community? What treasure might they contribute to the stream of life?

5. What is your treasure? How do you share it?

CLOSING

My feet ache from standing in the line for water,
Be with me, Holy Spirit.

My knees scrape the ground as I serve the meal,
Be with me, Holy Spirit.

Keep me hidden from the soldiers,
Be with me, Holy Spirit.

My child has no milk, protect my daughters,
Be with me, Holy Spirit.

Let me learn, let me use my brain,
Be with me, Holy Spirit.

I lean against the door and smell the fresh air that seeps through the cracks,

*My soul proclaims the greatness of the Lord, My spirit rejoices in God my Savior;
For he has looked with favor on his lowly servant. Amen.*

*Opening and Closing by Jo Trepagnier, Beijing Circle, Cathedral Church of the
Nativity, Bethlehem, Pennsylvania*

RESOURCES

The Geography of Faith: Underground Conversations on Religious, Political, and Social Change by Robert
  Coles and Daniel Berrigan (Woodstock, VT: SkyLight Paths, 2001). Lets you in on a dialogue between
  Coles and Berrigan on how they struggled with putting their faith into action.

Saints and Superheroes

SCRIPTURE REFERENCES

Isaiah 25:6–9

Wisdom 3:1–9

Revelation 21:2

John 11:1–44

OPENING

Holy One,

Draw my inner light of holiness to Your brightness

My meager spark toward your luxuriant flame

My glimmer of good toward Your beauty of holiness.

Turn me inside out!

Call me forth from my tomb of ignorance

That I might meet you openly upon love's slender path

Then send me, that I might be Your saint in this world.

DISCUSSION QUESTIONS

1. The words *whole* and *healed* form the roots of the word *holy*. What does it mean for a holy person to be someone whole? Someone healed?

2. A well-known hymn tells this about saints, "You can meet in school, or in lanes, or at sea, in the church or in trains, or in shops or at tea." Where is the most unexpected place you have met a saint? Why is she or he a saint?

3. How does knowing that you are part of a long procession of saints who have come before and saints who have yet to come change how you see yourself? How might you use this image to make decisions?

4. What does the image of a "spark running through stubble" suggest about God's call to us as agents of change?

5. Have you been turned inside out? Was it transforming? If so, how?

CLOSING

Holy One

Send me.

Let me be

one small and silent saint

in this vast and busy suffering world.

Opening and Closing by The Rev. Suzanne Guthrie,
www.edgeofenclosure.org

RESOURCES

Christ in the Margins by Robert Lentz (Maryknoll, NY: Orbis Books, 2003). Pairs icons by Robert Lentz with the stories of a variety of saints such as Harvey Milk and Albert Einstein.

Cloud of Witnesses by Jim Wallis and Joyce Hollyday (Maryknoll, NY: Orbis Books, 2005). Shares the lives of well-known and lesser-known saints, including Martin Luther King, Jr., Saint Francis of Assisi, and more.

Patrons and Protectors by Michael O'Neill McGrath (Chicago: Archdiocese of Chicago, 2007). Tells the stories of patron saints of the work of everyday people and how they might spark our lives. (A series written for older elementary school children that can also serve as daily readings for adults.)

Holy Conversation

Scripture References

Genesis 9:11–17

Mark 1:15

Acts 21:42

Romans 8:38–39

Opening

I breathe in slowly, deeply,

and hear your Spirit, birthing me afresh;

your Word, calling me good, sending me forth.

I breathe out slowly, deeply,

and offer in silence the prayers

your Spirit sighs within my heart,

the prayers you already know.

Beloved God,

I shall cherish this holy conversation

all the days of my breath,

and then, as long as we both shall live.

Amen.

Discussion Questions

1. When have you recently had a conversation as Jefferts Schori describes it, "encountering each other in a deep enough way to begin to see the image of God in (y)our neighbor"? What image of God did you see? What image of God was revealed in yourself?

2. Jefferts Schori paraphrases God's response to the flood that destroyed nearly everything with this, "Well, maybe I got it wrong. I won't do that again." How could believing in a God who admits mistakes change your relationship with God? What are the challenges to this belief?

3. What words or phrases would you use today to express the reality of your experience? Do the words surprise you? Have you ever been surprised by your prayers?

4. How would considering God's presence among us in Jesus as a *conversation* change your prayers and your actions?

CLOSING

Most gracious God, by our life on earth, you grant to each of us the gift of experiencing in community our holy and eternal conversation with you: Help us to encounter one another deeply, with mutual respect and careful listening, that as we speak truth in love to one another, each of us may be changed into your likeness, and this world transformed into the fullness of your reign. Amen.

Opening and Closing by The Rev. Jeanne Person, director, The Center for Christian Spirituality at General Theological Seminary

RESOURCES

Hearing from the Heart by Debra K. Farrington (San Francisco: Jossey-Bass, 2003). Guides the reader into ways of hearing the conversation with God.

Secrets of Prayer: A Multifaith Guide to Creating Personal Prayer in Your Life by Nancy Corcoran (Woodstock, VT: SkyLight Paths, 2008). Unlocks six secrets about what prayer actually is and shows you that prayer doesn't have to be perfect, it doesn't need formulas and it doesn't have to be planned.

Practicing Peace

SCRIPTURE REFERENCES

Isaiah 35:1–10

Ephesians 4:1–6

OPENING

Almighty God, we thank you for your unfailing love. You are so good to us, but we are not worthy. We have gone astray many times, in many ways. But your love and forgiveness remain constant. The sacrifice of your son is the weapon and the strength to fight for peace in this world.

Heal us from the effects of war, O God our Father. Give us the power of love and forgiveness that we may forgive those who have wronged us and live in harmony and peace with them.

DISCUSSION QUESTIONS

1. When is that last time you encountered rage in someone? How did you respond? In reflection, would you respond differently? Why or why not?

2. A paradox is a statement that is true, yet appears not to be true. What insight reveals the truth of Jesus' seemingly paradoxical response to violence? Can that insight be taught or must it be experienced to understand the paradox?

3. When is the last time you were angry? What prompted your anger? How did you respond? In reflection, would you respond differently? Why or why not?

4. Considering the stories in this chapter, what role does power play in anger? Why does power matter to peace?

5. Imagine a world without violence. What would it look like? What actions does your imagination suggest are needed to get there?

CLOSING

We pray for all who are weak and helpless, especially widows and widowers, orphans, the disabled, and the elderly who have lost their sons and daughters during the war and are now left lonely and hopeless. Restore their hopes, O God.

We pray for the spirit of tolerance and perseverance in the work of your Church, O God.

We pray for our leaders and the rest of the world leaders. Bless them with the spirit of love. Give them skills of good leadership so that there will be peace all over the world.

Bring to us peace that can change the whole world for the better living of your people.

We pray this in the name of our Lord Jesus Christ. Amen.

Opening and Closing by Betty Kojo, Mother's Union, Kajo Keji, Sudan

RESOURCES

Fellowship for Reconciliation (forusa.org). The website of a group of women and men who seek to respond to conflict nonviolently and through compassionate action.

Living Peace by John Dear (New York: Image, 2004). Presents reflections by Dear from his own life about how to bring peace to one's self and the world.

Pentecost Continues

SCRIPTURE REFERENCES

John 16:12–13

Acts 2:1–4

Acts: 2:11

OPENING

Almighty God, you have created a vast and glorious Tent of Meeting for your people throughout the earth. Help us to remember you have invited all to dwell here with you.

All are welcome in this place.

Guide the hearts of those working to enlarge the tent of your Church with acts of your Love—with hospitality, compassion and acceptance.

All are welcome in this place.

Bless the hands of those mending the rents in your Church and weaving your Love into the fibers of the warp and weft to strengthen the fabric of your earthly family.

All are welcome in this place.

Remind us that we are tenants and not the landlords of your Church. Guide us with your Spirit to share equally, love unconditionally and respect all.

All are welcome in this place.

Continue to send your Spirit among us so we may hear your Voice and do your Will as the people of your Church, the children of your Heart.

All are One. All are welcome in this place. Amen.

Discussion Questions

1. Has the Spirit ever found you despite your being hunkered down behind closed doors? What did the Spirit say to you?

2. What are the tensions within your faith community? What truth is held in that tension?

3. What are the promises and challenges of being in dialogue among those who hear the Spirit differently?

4. What does the value of self-determination suggest about ecumenical and interfaith dialogue?

5. How might diversity maintain health within a community?

Closing

Good and Gracious God, in this time of uncertainly, change and turmoil, we seek your holy inspiration, eternal wisdom, and divine words. Fill these our earthly tents with your Spirit of truth, compassion, mercy, and kindness. With the power of your Holy Spirit, scatter far the dust of old prejudices, hurts, and fears; and clear the cobwebs from our hearts and minds so we may grasp your vision for your people. Speak to us as you spoke to the prophets and help us to bear what we need to hear. Give us the strength, the clarity, and the courage to be what you would have us be and to do your will and your work in this world. All this we ask for your children's sake. Amen.

Opening and closing by Pamela RW Kandt, St. Mark's Episcopal Church, Casper, Wyoming

Resources

Listening Hearts (www.listeninghearts.org). Teaches ways of listening for communities seeking to discern what the Spirit continues to say and call to them.

Living the Questions

SCRIPTURE REFERENCES

Matthew 10:39

OPENING

Lord Jesus Christ, you emptied yourself, taking the form of a servant that we might know the truth of the nature of God. Give us grace that we might embrace the mystery of limitation and learn more fully that patience with paradox can lead us to a deep reality hidden from our eyes. Help us to cling to you now, trusting that in time all will know the power and justice of your love for all your children. Amen.

DISCUSSION QUESTIONS

1. Every baptized person is meant to be involved in ministry. What ministry do you have inside the church? Outside the church?

2. Where does your ministry take place? What signs of God's kingdom do you see there?

3. When did your adult journey of faith begin? How has it shaped you today?

4. What big questions are you living?

CLOSING

Holy Spirit, your gentle laughter echoes throughout the halls of creation, wiping away our tears and transforming all our shame into glory. Shower us with courage to follow your steps in the dance of our lives that we might trust that you will lead us to where we must be, even if it seems for a moment to take us to a place of darkness and despair. For you are Light and in you we shall see the truth. Amen.

Opening and Closing by The Very Rev. Nicholas Knisely, dean,
Trinity Cathedral, Phoenix, Arizona

RESOURCES

Hearing the Call across Traditions: Readings on Faith and Service edited by Adam Davis; foreword by Eboo Patel (Woodstock, VT: SkyLight Paths, 2009). Explores the connections between faith, service and social justice through the prose, verse and sacred texts of the world's great faith traditions—Christianity, Judaism, Islam, Buddhism, Hinduism, Taoism, and more.

A Hidden Wholeness: The Journey Toward an Undivided Life by Parker Palmer (San Francisco: Jossey-Bass, 2004). Helps you discern your baptismal ministry by listening to your life and hearing the call within community. Our hidden wholeness is when our actions match our values.

High Anxiety

SCRIPTURE REFERENCES

Matthew 28

Luke 28:18

Jon 20:26

John 21:9–13

OPENING

O Creator God, you wrap the whole world in a loving embrace; help us to let go of our fears and our anxiety, and instill in their stead hope beyond imagining, so that we may bring about your commonwealth here on earth. Amen.

DISCUSSION QUESTIONS

1. How does Jesus instill fear in your everyday life? How does Jesus bring peace to your life?

2. How might anxiety in interfaith circles be diffused? What is the promise of addressing that anxiety?

3. What do you fear in your life? Which fears are legitimate? Which fears might be driven by society as a way to gain a false sense of security?

4. Some claim that Christians emphasize orthodoxy far more than do other faith traditions. Do you agree or disagree with this claim? What are the promises and challenges of emphasizing orthodoxy in our pluralistic world?

5. What other faith traditions do not seem "normal" to you? How might you see them as normal in both your mind and heart?

CLOSING

Ever-loving God, you made us in your image and love us like a mother; take away the fears that paralyze us, and in their place give us hope; take away the anxiety that stills our hands, and in its stead give us passion for justice, so that we might be mid-wives of the coming of your kingdom. Amen.

Opening and Closing by The Rev. Mariclair Partee, canon for the Ministry of the Baptized, The Cathedral Church of the Nativity, Bethlehem, Pennsylvania

RESOURCES

Following Jesus in a Culture of Fear by Scott Bader-Saye (Grand Rapids, MI: Brazos Press, 2007). Challenges us to draw on providence to transform anxiety to courage.

Pushing the Boundaries

SCRIPTURE REFERENCES

Mark 3:21

Luke 1:39–50

Romans 4:13–25

OPENING

Dear God, we do not worship as we should, with total trust in your love. We create laws and boundaries for ourselves, and we place our faith in the traditions and rituals we have created by the work of our hands.

Teach us to let go and to seek only nearness to you. Grant that we might live as your son Jesus lived, who trusted so wholly in you that not even the words of his own parents kept him from your house.

Loving God, may we know that we are your children, and that you alone are our Father, Amen.

DISCUSSION QUESTIONS

1. How do children push the boundaries that are set for them?

2. How do children bring you closer to the kingdom of God?

3. Who are your enemies? Does God really call you to love them? Why or why not? What might this love look like?

4. How do you continue to grow by taking risks and experiencing failure?

5. How is your community listening to the young adults in your midst? What do you hear them say that "sends you screaming into the night"? What new life is emerging from their voices?

CLOSING

Lord Jesus, we are afraid of what we do not know, and any future that we have not created terrifies us. But you, Lord, have gone before us, and the stone on our tomb is rolled away.

Today we are your body in the world. Give us the courage to rise daily with you in the Resurrection. Give us the humility to learn from the communion of saints who have gone on before, and to trust in those who will come after.

Lord Jesus, be a lamp unto our feet, that we who are the Church of today will not fear what we have not imagined, and as we move forward give us the grace to trust that you are already at work in every possible future. Amen.

Opening and Closing by Daniel Strandlund, sr. high youth minister,
St. Stephen's Episcopal Church, Birmingham, Alabama

RESOURCES

Emerging Churches by Eddie Gibbs and Ryan K. Bolger (Grand Rapids, MI: Baker Books, 2005). Encourages traditionalists to listen to new ways of "being church."

God Within: Our Spiritual Future—As Told by Today's New Adults edited by Jon M. Sweeney and the Editors at SkyLight Paths (Woodstock, VT: SkyLight Paths, 2003). This thought-provoking collection of writings, poetry, and art showcases the voices that are defining the future of religion, faith, and belief as we know it.

Unchristian: What a New Generation Thinks about Christianity by Dave Kinnaman (Grand Rapids, MI: Baker Books, 2008). Gives you a glimpse into young people's impressions of the church by interspersing sound research with interviews of young people today.

Go Forth for God

OPENING

God of tradition and change, give us new eyes to go forth into the world expecting to encounter the movement of the Spirit in new places. Help us to hear the big questions of those who seek meaning in their lives. Embolden us to embark on new places in the name of God's son who continues to emerge among us.

DISCUSSION QUESTIONS

1. How does your church evangelize? What motivates that evangelism?

2. Many Christians have moved from one denomination to another. What does this suggest about how your community "does church"?

3. How is God challenging you to embark on "new territory and experience God in new situations"? How is this rooted in tradition? How is it leading to new traditions?

4. What questions keep your church alive? Who is asking these questions? Who is listening?

CLOSING

Loving God, grant us the clarity to see the face of Jesus in all who cross my path today. To recognize your sacred presence in all is to live a richer life of hope, grace, and integrity. May we remember that we are created in your image, worthy of honor and respect, and called to action through your love.

Opening and Closing by Lydia Kelsey Bucklin, missioner for the Diocese of Iowa and a young adult

RESOURCES

Being (www.onbeing.org), formerly Speaking of Faith, explores issues of faith from a variety of perspectives, both sacred and secular. Available as a podcast.

Episcopal Church Visual Arts (www.ecva.org). Exhibits works by Episcopal artists. Reflecting on art offers a contemporary way of understanding Jesus in the world.

WingClips (www.wingclips). Lists contemporary films by theme. These clips can serve as the basis of conversations of faith.

Fossils

SCRIPTURE REFERENCES

Genesis 12:1

Zecharaiah 8:12

Mark 10:45–47

Luke 9:23

OPENING

O God, sometimes I feel like I am fossilized. I feel stuck, mired in the past or in the struggles and poverty of the present, or frozen by fear of what lies ahead. I sometimes feel that I am worth nothing. Help me to learn from these experiences and be unhinged from them long enough that I might, with your help and the help of a community of others, take the risk to venture into the waters of life with all of its tears, hopes, and promise. As I know that my journey in faith is to move from rooms filled with fear in order to enter other rooms filled with fear, give me the strength and the will to do it.

DISCUSSION QUESTIONS

1. What is the mission statement of your faith community?

2. What are your faith community's dreams for the world?

3. Where might your community be fossilizing? What could be done to undo this process?

4. What does the breath of God feel like? What does it prompt you to do?

CLOSING

I dare contemplate making this journey because I know that you have gone before, will stay the journey with me, and are waiting at my next way station to stir up new life, forgiveness, healing, justice, love, and hope. What I ask for myself I also yearn for others. With gratitude that exceeds any words I might use and a commitment that is larger than a promise, I offer myself this day in thanksgiving for your love and prodding to bring us all to new creative, redemptive life.

Opening and Closing by Bud Holland, priest, Diocese of Pennsylvania

RESOURCES

Christianity for the Rest of Us by Diana Butler Bass (San Francisco: HarperCollins, 2006). Discusses ten signposts of renewal revealed in her study of churches with vitality.

What If Starbucks Marketed Like a Church? A Parable by Richard Reising (YouTube, 2008). Might help your community respond to changes in culture without sacrificing core values.

A Moveable Feast

SCRIPTURE REFERENCES

Luke 7:36–50

Galatians 2:18

1 John 4:18

OPENING

Blessed be God the Word who came to his own and his own received him not, for in this way God glorifies the stranger; O God show us your image in all who come to us today, that we may welcome them and you. Amen.

DISCUSSION QUESTIONS

1. What acts of hospitality does your faith community need to do to unlock its "inside language" to those who are walking into your doors for the first time?

2. How does your church minister to alcoholics, drug addicts, gambling addicts, prostitutes, and other "untouchables" in a way that invites them into a deep relationship with your community?

3. It is surprising to hear that "[i]t's actually our fear of the wretchedness within our own souls that pushes us away from our sisters and brothers." How might this be true for you?

4. What are your veneers?

CLOSING

O God, you bring outcasts along with you wherever you go, and tear through the tissue of our well-mannered lives so that we must change our plans. Increase in us the gift of love matched with courage to welcome the mystery of your presence in those we don't expect and rejoice to be changed by strangers. Help us to depend on uninvited guests and rowdy tablemates so that when we join you at your heavenly banquet we may not turn away, but join them in the scandalous feast. We make our prayer through Jesus Christ, crashing every party. Amen.

Opening from a prayer attributed to Gregory of Nazianzus (c. 329–390) and used at the beginning of worship at the Church of St. Gregory of Nyssa, San Francisco

Closing prayer by The Rev. Paul D. Fromberg © 2010

RESOURCES

Babette's Feast (movie directed by Gabriel Axel, 1987). The story of the transformation of a closed community that embraces the outsider over a shared meal.

Radical Welcome: Embracing God, the Other, and the Spirit of Transformation by Stephanie Spellers (New York: Church Publishing, 2006). Lifts up the possibility of a church of authentic inclusivity told through stories of congregations across the country.

Healing Division

SCRIPTURE REFERENCES

Mark 1:29–31

Mark 5:43

Luke 17:11–19

1 Corinthians 9:16–18

OPENING

Gracious God, who embraced the limits of humankind by taking on our form in your son, help us to embrace our common humanity when we can't seem to agree on anything else, help us to find unity in our woundedness as we strive to see across our divisions, help us to grow into more abundant life through our shared resurrection in Jesus. Amen.

DISCUSSION QUESTIONS

1. When have you found new life? What lifted you from the depths of death and despair?

2. How have people who are differently-abled blessed your community? In what ways has your community welcomed their blessings?

3. Have you been healed in ways that have brought you more wholly into community? How?

4. Has your pain led you to a generosity in abundance? If so, how? If not, what do you need to do so?

CLOSING

Ever Creating God, who made us one people and one body; give us the vision, in our diversity, to see that we are all protected under the shadow of your wings, and out of the warmth of that shared embrace let us find the courage and strength to serve one another, all to the glory of your name. Amen.

Opening and Closing by The Rev. Mariclair Partee, canon for the Ministry of the Baptized, The Cathedral Church of the Nativity, Bethlehem, Pennsylvania

RESOURCES

Beyond Accessibility: Toward Full Inclusion of People with Disabilities in Faith Communities by Brett Webb-Mitchell (NY: Church Publishing, 2010). Argues for the full inclusion of all people in the body of Christ.

Finding God in Dissent

SCRIPTURE REFERENCES

Genesis 22:17

Luke 8:50

Luke 13:31–34

OPENING

God, who loves each of us beyond imagining even when hostility is present among us, be with us. When we are with those with whom we cannot agree: help us to listen carefully with our hearts as well as with our minds, speak respectfully, and understand with compassion their words and actions. Help us to heal our broken past and to move forward together—carefully, respectfully, and compassionately—with hope for a wholeness that we may know through your grace. Amen.

DISCUSSION QUESTIONS

1. What does the image of a hen gathering her chicks under her wings say to you?

2. How does seeing a tyrant as a fox change the dynamics of relationships in the church?

3. Where is the fox lurking in your community? What gift of God gives you shelter from the foxes?

CLOSING

God, where are you when the only voice I want to hear is my own? Grant me strength and courage to listen for your voice as I listen to others today. Help me to know that my voice is not the only right way. Amen.

Opening and Closing by Debbi Rodahaffer, director of Christian education,
St. Matthew's Episcopal Church, Louisville, Kentucky

Resources

"Hope" from *The Long Way* by the Dixie Chicks (Sony, 2006). The Dixie Chicks sing of hope to live fearlessly in a world of joy, laughter, and love. Read the lyrics and consider what is says about God's dreams.

About the Author

A popular speaker, retreat leader, and workshop presenter on the topics of spirituality, prayer, and teen faith formation, **Jenifer Gamber** has been involved in Christian formation since she began teaching Sunday school as a teenager. She is the author of two widely read books about religious formation: *My Faith, My Life* for teenagers and *Your Faith, Your Life* for adults. Her website, www.myfaithmylife.org, offers a wealth of resources for adults who work with youth. She is the vice president of the National Association for Episcopal Christian Education Directors, and has an active ministry leading confirmation and baptism preparation at her home church, the Cathedral Church of the Nativity in Bethlehem, Pennsylvania.

Printed in the USA
CPSIA information can be obtained
at www.ICGtesting.com
JSHW060048150824
68134JS00031B/2670

9 781594 733086